THE WAY OF THE
MARKSMEN
STUDY GUIDE

Copyright © 2025 by Richard Hernandez

Published by Arrows & Stones

All rights reserved. No portion of this book may be reproduced, stored in a retrieval system, or transmitted in any form or by any means—electronic, mechanical, photocopy, recording, scanning, or other—except for brief quotations in critical reviews or articles, without prior written permission of the author.

Scripture quotations marked NIV are taken from the Holy Bible, New International Version®, NIV®. Copyright © 1973, 1978, 1984, 2011 by Biblica, Inc.™ Used by permission of Zondervan. All rights reserved worldwide. www.zondervan.com. The "NIV" and "New International Version" are trademarks registered in the United States Patent and Trademark Office by Biblica, Inc.™ | Scripture quotations marked NLT are taken from the Holy Bible, New Living Translation, copyright © 1996, 2004, 2015 by Tyndale House Foundation. Used by permission of Tyndale House Publishers, Inc., Carol Stream, Illinois 60188. All rights reserved.

For foreign and subsidiary rights, contact the author.

Cover design by Sara Young

ISBN: 978-1-964794-46-4   1 2 3 4 5 6 7 8 9 10

Printed in the United States of America

STUDY GUIDE

THE WAY OF THE
MARKSMEN

RICHARD
HERNANDEZ

CONTENTS

Introduction 6

PART 1. **The Way of a Marksman** 9

    CHAPTER 1. **North: Put God First** 10

    CHAPTER 2. **South: Deny Yourself** 16

    CHAPTER 3. **East: Part A: Value Family** 22

    CHAPTER 4. **West: Part B: Uphold Ministry** 28

PART 2. **The Measure of a Marksman** 35

    CHAPTER 5. **The Fear of God** 36

    CHAPTER 6. **Know the Word** 42

    CHAPTER 7. **Mature as Men** 48

    CHAPTER 8. **Know who You Are** 54

    CHAPTER 9. **Be Like Jesus** 60

PART 3. **The Character of a Marksman** 67

    CHAPTER 10. **Men of Integrity** 68

    CHAPTER 11. **Men of Humility** 74

    CHAPTER 12. **Men of Courage** 80

    CHAPTER 13. **Men of Compassion** 86

    CHAPTER 14. **Men of Faith** 92

    CHAPTER 15. **It All Comes Together** 98

INTRODUCTION

EACH CHAPTER INCLUDES:

Icebreaker—A discussion starter to help engage the group.

Discussion Tips—Guidelines to encourage honest reflection and meaningful conversation.

Closing Challenge—A personal action step to apply the lesson.

This book is designed for both **personal reflection** and **meaningful group discussions**. As you go through each chapter with other men, take time to **openly share insights, challenges, and victories**. Use the reflection questions to spark conversations that build **accountability and growth**.

The goal isn't just to **gain knowledge**—it's to **live it out**. These principles are meant to shape your daily life, helping you stay on course as you follow Jesus. **Be honest, listen well, and challenge each other** to live the way of the Marksmen outlined in the book.

HOW TO USE THIS STUDY GUIDE AS A GROUP

Each chapter includes:
- **Icebreaker**—A discussion starter to help engage the group.
- **Discussion Tips**—Guidelines to encourage honest reflection and meaningful conversation.
- **Closing Challenge**—A personal action step to apply the lesson.

Throughout the study, keep these key principles in mind:
- Encourage honesty without judgment.
- Ask follow-up questions to dig deeper.
- Use the **compass illustration** to reinforce the theme.
- End each session with a practical step to apply the teaching.

PART 1

THE WAY OF A MARKSMAN

CHAPTER 1

NORTH: PUT GOD FIRST

> Blood, sweat, and tears may be the currency by which wisdom is purchased.

READING TIME

As you read Chapter 1: "North: Put God First" in *The Way of the Marksmen*, review, reflect on, and respond to the text by answering the following questions.

REVIEW, REFLECT, AND RESPOND

Reflect on a time when you thought God was first in your life, but your actions said otherwise. What was holding you back from fully prioritizing Him?

_____

_____

_____

_____

_____

_____

_____

_____

Reflect on the statement: "*Actions will always speak louder than words.*" What specific actions in your life demonstrate that God is first? Where do you need to realign your priorities?

_____

_____

_____

_____

_____

_____

_____

_____

> "Looking at the man, Jesus felt genuine love for him. 'There is still one thing you haven't done,' he told him. 'Go and sell all your possessions and give the money to the poor, and you will have treasure in heaven. Then come, follow me.' At this, the man's face fell, and he went away sad, for he had many possessions."
>
> —Mark 10:21-22 (NLT)

Consider the scripture above and answer the following questions:

If Jesus asked you to let go of something valuable in your life today, how would you respond? What emotions or fears might surface?

_____
_____
_____
_____
_____
_____
_____

What are the "possessions" or comforts in your life that prevent you from fully following Jesus? Why are they hard to let go of?

_____
_____
_____
_____
_____
_____
_____
_____

What "harmless hobbies" or interests have you allowed to take God's rightful place in your heart?

_____
_____
_____
_____
_____
_____

Consider Gideon's story in Judges 6, where he had to tear down idols in his community. What steps can you take to identify and tear down the idols in your life or home?

_____
_____
_____
_____
_____
_____
_____

James encourages us to ask God for wisdom when we lack direction (James 1:5). In what areas of your life do you need God's wisdom to navigate your path?

_____
_____
_____
_____
_____
_____

How do unresolved emotions, such as anger or pride, reveal areas where God is not fully first in your life? What can you do to surrender those emotions to Him?

_____
_____
_____
_____
_____
_____
_____
_____

The author mentions that "following Jesus has a price." What sacrifices have you made in following Jesus, and how has God honored those sacrifices in your life?

_____
_____
_____
_____
_____
_____
_____
_____

The chapter uses a compass illustration for finding "True North" in life. What practical steps can you take this week to keep your eyes fixed on Jesus as your True North?

_____
_____
_____
_____
_____
_____
_____
_____
_____

Icebreaker: Lost and Found—Share a time when you got lost—physically or spiritually. How did you find your way back? How did that experience shape you?

Discussion Tips: See "How to Use This Study Guide" for general guidelines.
- Discuss how distractions in life can make it difficult to keep God as our True North.
- Challenge the group to consider what it looks like to truly put God first in daily decisions?

Closing Challenge: Identify one area where you need to put God first this week. Take action and check in next time.

CHAPTER 2

SOUTH: DENY YOURSELF

> No matter how far off track we've gotten, there's always a way back to Jesus if we're willing to run toward Him.

READING TIME

As you read Chapter 2: "South: Deny Yourself" in *The Way of the Marksmen*, review, reflect on, and respond to the text by answering the following questions.

REVIEW, REFLECT, AND RESPOND

Reflect on a time when you found it difficult to let go of control and fully surrender to God's will. What was the outcome, and what did you learn from that experience?

_____
_____
_____
_____
_____
_____
_____

There is a big difference between self-denial and self-righteousness. Have you ever made sacrifices with the wrong motives? How did that impact your relationship with God and others?

_____
_____
_____
_____
_____
_____
_____
_____

> "Throw off your old sinful nature and your former way of life, which is corrupted by lust and deception. Instead, let the Spirit renew your thoughts and attitudes. Put on your new nature, created to be like God—truly righteous and holy."
>
> —Ephesians 4:22-24 [NLT]

Consider the scripture above and answer the following questions:

Reflect on the phrase, *"Let the Spirit renew your thoughts and attitudes."* In what areas of your thinking or perspective do you most need God's renewal right now?

_____
_____
_____
_____
_____
_____
_____

What aspects of your "old sinful nature" still linger in your life? What's keeping you from "throwing them off" and allowing God to transform you?

_____
_____
_____
_____
_____
_____
_____

Peter struggled with self-denial, from his rebuke of Jesus to his eventual denial of Him. How does Peter's journey resonate with your own struggles in surrendering to God's plan?

_____

_____

_____

_____

_____

_____

_____

Reflect on a moment when you "compared your calling" to someone else's, as Peter did with John. How did comparison impact your focus and ability to follow God's will?

_____

_____

_____

_____

_____

_____

_____

Self-denial is not about perfectionism but about transformation. In what ways can perfectionism hinder your spiritual growth and surrender to God?

_____

_____

_____

_____

_____

_____

Have you ever felt burdened by religious rules? Where do you think this came from, and what role does it play in your life today?

_____
_____
_____
_____
_____
_____
_____
_____

What has the process of sanctification looked like in your own life and journey with God? Are you satisfied with where you are now? Why or why not?

_____
_____
_____
_____
_____
_____
_____
_____
_____

In what ways have you attempted to redefine what a "man of God" looks like in order to fit your own desires and expectations or justify your behaviors?

_____
_____
_____
_____
_____
_____
_____
_____

Icebreaker: Letting Go—Share a time when you had to give up something you wanted for the sake of something greater. How did that decision affect you? Did it bring regret or growth?

Discussion Tips: See "How to Use This Study Guide" for general guidelines.
- Discuss why self-denial is difficult and how it counters today's culture of self-promotion.
- Encourage the group to reflect on how denying oneself can lead to spiritual freedom rather than restriction.

Closing Challenge: Identify one area where you need to deny yourself this week in order to follow Jesus more fully. Take action and check in next time.

CHAPTER 3

EAST: PART A: VALUE FAMILY

> There is no higher calling for a man than to be about his family and God's extended family.

READING TIME

As you read Chapter 3: "East: Part A: Value Family" in *The Way of the Marksmen*, review, reflect on, and respond to the text by answering the following questions.

REVIEW, REFLECT, AND RESPOND

Valuing family is about responsibility, commitment, and leadership. How are you currently fulfilling these roles in your family, and where do you feel you need to improve?

_____
_____
_____
_____
_____
_____
_____

Reflect on the statement: *"A man's failure to lead spiritually opens the door to confusion and division."* Why do you think poor leadership sows seeds of confusion and division? How are they related?

_____
_____
_____
_____
_____
_____
_____

> *"In the same way, you husbands must give honor to your wives. Treat your wife with understanding as you live together. She may be weaker than you are, but she is your equal partner in God's gift of new life. Treat her as you should so your prayers will not be hindered."*
>
> —1 Peter 3:7 (NLT)

Consider the scripture above and answer the following questions:

In what ways does this scripture mirror the dynamics of your relationship with your wife? What does "giving honor" to your wife encompass?

_____
_____
_____
_____
_____
_____
_____

How does equal partnership play out practically in your marriage? What strengths does your spouse have that you may be overlooking? How can you intentionally honor and support her in those areas?

_____
_____
_____
_____
_____
_____

Adam failed to protect his family in the Garden of Eden. In what ways do you see the consequences of neglecting family leadership in today's culture or your own life?

_____
_____
_____
_____
_____
_____

What is one practical way you could demonstrate sacrificial love to your spouse or loved ones this week?

_____
_____
_____
_____
_____
_____

What challenges do you regularly encounter in raising your children in the Lord, and how can you address those obstacles intentionally?

_____
_____
_____
_____
_____
_____

What past wounds or patterns in your life affect how you relate to your family today? What are you doing to heal them?

_____
_____
_____
_____
_____
_____
_____
_____
_____

How does comparison with other families affect your view of your own? Are you allowing unrealistic expectations to influence how you lead, love, or nurture your family?

_____
_____
_____
_____
_____
_____
_____
_____
_____

Think about the way you spend your time at home. Are you physically present but emotionally absent? What is one area where you can become more intentional in engaging with your family?

_____
_____
_____
_____
_____
_____
_____
_____

Icebreaker: Family Legacy—Share a lesson about family that was passed down to you. How has that shaped the way you lead and invest in your family today?

Discussion Tips: See "How to Use This Study Guide" for general guidelines.
- Talk about how leadership in the family impacts spiritual growth.
- Discuss how modern distractions can pull men away from leading and valuing family.

Closing Challenge: Identify one way you can **intentionally honor, lead, or invest in your family** this week—whether through time, words, or actions. Take action and check in next time.

CHAPTER 4

WEST: PART B: UPHOLD MINISTRY

> We need to be careful not to let our expectations of recognition define our fulfillment.

READING TIME

As you read Chapter 4: "West: Part B: Uphold Ministry" in *The Way of the Marksmen*, review, reflect on, and respond to the text by answering the following questions.

REVIEW, REFLECT, AND RESPOND

Reflect on the statement: *"Your home is your first ministry, but the advancement of the gospel is a critical calling and responsibility."* Have you ever prioritized ministry work over your family? What were the consequences, and how can you find a healthier balance?

_____
_____
_____
_____
_____
_____
_____
_____
_____

Have you ever struggled with mixed motives in your service? How can you ensure your focus remains on serving God and others?

_____
_____
_____
_____
_____
_____
_____

> "For even the Son of Man came not to be served but to serve others and to give his life as a ransom for many."
>
> —Mark 10:45 (NLT)

Consider the scripture above and answer the following questions:

Jesus modeled servant leadership by putting others' needs before His own. In what areas of your life do you find it difficult to serve selflessly? What holds you back?

_____

_____

_____

_____

_____

_____

_____

_____

Reflect on a time when you served someone without recognition or reward. How did that experience deepen your understanding of Christ's sacrificial love?

_____

_____

_____

_____

_____

_____

_____

_____

When have you felt discouraged by a lack of appreciation for your efforts? How did you respond, and what did you learn?

In what ways have you used ministry and serving to fill a void rather than relying on God for your identity?

What areas of ministry or service feel unseen or underappreciated? How can you find encouragement in knowing that God rewards faithfulness?

Paul warns in Philippians 1:17 about those who preach with selfish ambition. How can you guard your heart against pride, self-promotion, or comparison in your ministry?

_____

_____

_____

_____

_____

_____

_____

_____

_____

_____

Have you ever persevered in ministry when the impact wasn't clear? How did God sustain you, and what did you learn from that season?

_____

_____

_____

_____

_____

_____

_____

_____

_____

_____

Reflect on this challenge: *"Ministry means serving those who can give you nothing in return."* Whom in your life might God be calling you to serve sacrificially right now, and how can you take a step toward doing so?

_____
_____
_____
_____
_____
_____
_____
_____

Icebreaker: Serving Without Recognition—Share a time when you put in effort or served in some way but received little or no recognition. How did that experience affect your mindset about serving?

Discussion Tips: See "How to Use This Study Guide" for general guidelines.
- Discuss why serving in ministry must be rooted in humility rather than recognition.
- Challenge the group to reflect on whether they are serving from a place of love or obligation?

Closing Challenge: Identify one way you can serve selflessly this week—whether in your home, workplace, or ministry—without expecting recognition. Take action and check in next time.

PART 2
THE MEASURE OF A MARKSMAN

CHAPTER 5

THE FEAR OF GOD

> The fear of God starts us on this journey, and once we lose it, we will miss the target entirely.

READING TIME

As you read Chapter 5: "The Fear of God" in *The Way of the Marksmen*, review, reflect on, and respond to the text by answering the following questions.

REVIEW, REFLECT, AND RESPOND

How does the fear of God show up in your life? In what ways might you be taking your calling to represent God for granted?

_____
_____
_____
_____
_____
_____
_____
_____

Reflect on a time when you acted out of fear of people's opinions rather than fear of God. What were the consequences, and what changes have you made since then?

_____
_____
_____
_____
_____
_____
_____
_____

> "There is no fear in love, but perfect love casts out fear. For fear has to do with punishment, and whoever fears has not been perfected in love."
>
> —1 John 4:18 (ESV)

Consider the scripture above and answer the following questions:

In what ways are you still holding onto fears that contradict God's love? What lies or misconceptions about God's character might be feeding those fears, and how does this scripture challenge those beliefs?

_____
_____
_____
_____
_____
_____
_____
_____

How does fear of punishment hinder you from loving, serving, and leading well?

_____
_____
_____
_____
_____
_____
_____

In what areas of your life are you clinging to control instead of surrendering fully to God? What are you afraid might happen if you let go, and how does that stand up to scripture?

_____
_____
_____
_____
_____
_____

Reflect on a specific time when you experienced the consequences of ignoring God's direction or warnings. How did that experience shape your understanding of His authority and your need to fear Him rightly?

_____
_____
_____
_____
_____
_____

Why do you think obedience comes naturally out of the fear of the Lord? In what areas of your life do you find obedience to God the most challenging?

_____
_____
_____
_____
_____
_____

Contrasts are made between the fear of God and the fear of man. Who or what do you tend to "fear" more than God (e.g., approval, failure, rejection)? How can you begin to dismantle displaced fear and reassign it to God?

_____
_____
_____
_____
_____
_____
_____
_____

If you were to paint a mental picture of what the fear of God looks like, what would you see? What aspects of your personal relationship with God inspired that picture?

_____
_____
_____
_____
_____
_____
_____
_____

Complete the "Reverence Check" exercise at the end of this chapter. What did you discover, and how do you plan to move forward in pursuing the holy fear of God?

_____
_____
_____
_____
_____
_____
_____
_____

Icebreaker: Fear vs. Reverence—Share a time when you mistook fear for reverence or struggled to understand the difference. How did that experience shape your view of God?

Discussion Tips: See "How to Use This Study Guide" for general guidelines.
- Discuss how the fear of God differs from fear of punishment and how it leads to wisdom.
- Challenge the group to think about how fear of man impacts their decisions more than fear of God.

Closing Challenge: Identify one area where fear of man or personal control has taken priority over the fear of God in your life. Take a step this week to surrender that area fully to Him and check in next time.

CHAPTER 6

KNOW THE WORD

> You don't have to be a scholar; just be open to learning and growing. God will do the rest.

READING TIME

As you read Chapter 6: "Know the Word" in *The Way of the Marksmen*, review, reflect on, and respond to the text by answering the following questions.

REVIEW, REFLECT, AND RESPOND

What specific distractions or habits make it difficult for you to spend time in Scripture, and how can you intentionally replace one of those habits this week?

_____
_____
_____
_____
_____
_____
_____
_____

Reflect on a time when a specific verse or passage of Scripture brought clarity, comfort, or conviction. What was the situation, and how did that passage help you take a practical next step or make a critical decision?

_____
_____
_____
_____
_____
_____
_____
_____

> *"Your word is a lamp to guide my feet and a light for my path."*
>
> —Psalm 119:105 (NLT)

Consider the scripture above and answer the following questions:

Reflect on a time when you ignored the guidance of God's Word and chose your own path. What were the consequences, and how can you use this scripture and others to ensure you don't repeat that mistake?

_____
_____
_____
_____
_____
_____
_____
_____

Lamps provide light for only the next few steps, not the whole journey. Why do you think God shields us from seeing the full picture as we travel towards our destination? How is this applicable to your life right now?

_____
_____
_____
_____
_____
_____
_____
_____

What specific lie or temptation have you been wrestling with lately, and what passage of Scripture can you use to confront it directly?

_____
_____
_____
_____
_____
_____

Reflect on a time when you misinterpreted or misused Scripture. What were the ramifications, and how can you now approach Bible study with greater care and understanding to avoid a similar mistake?

_____
_____
_____
_____
_____
_____

What is one passage or teaching you've heard recently but struggled to live out? What's the first practical action you can take this week to apply it?

_____
_____
_____
_____
_____
_____

Scripture often reveals uncomfortable truths. Think about a recent passage that exposed an area of sin, pride, or avoidance in your life. What do you think God was showing you? How did you respond?

_____

_____

_____

_____

_____

Choose one verse this week to memorize. Why does this verse stand out to you, and how can it help you with a specific situation you're currently facing?

_____

_____

_____

_____

_____

Identify one specific habit, attitude, or relationship in your life that needs to change. What passage of Scripture speaks to this area, and how can you begin to act on it this week?

_____

_____

_____

_____
_____
_____

Complete the "Word Check" exercise at the end of this chapter. What did you discover, and how do you plan to move forward in becoming more familiar with the Word of God and applying it to your life?

_____
_____
_____
_____
_____

Icebreaker: Guided by the Word—Share a time when a specific Bible verse helped you through a difficult situation. How did it guide, challenge, or encourage you?

Discussion Tips: See "How to Use This Study Guide" for general guidelines.
- Talk about common distractions that prevent men from regularly reading Scripture.
- Encourage the group to discuss how applying the Word changes decision-making.

Closing Challenge: Choose one Bible verse to memorize this week and apply it to a specific area of your life. Be ready to share how it impacted you at the next meeting.

CHAPTER 7

MATURE AS MEN

> Jesus defines our possibilities,
> not the world.

READING TIME

As you read Chapter 7: "Mature as Men" in *The Way of the Marksmen*, review, reflect on, and respond to the text by answering the following questions.

REVIEW, REFLECT, AND RESPOND

Spiritual and emotional maturity often takes longer than we expect. How do you respond when you don't see the change you desire right away? Provide an example, and describe how your expectations have evolved over time.

_____
_____
_____
_____
_____
_____
_____

What might you be carrying with you from childhood that is hindering you from growing into a fully mature man of God? In what ways are you confronting those issues, and are they helping you or harming you? What should you do instead?

_____
_____
_____
_____
_____
_____
_____
_____

> "When I was a child, I spoke and thought and reasoned as a child. But when I grew up, I put away childish things."
>
> —1 Corinthians 13:11 (NLT)

Consider the scripture above and answer the following questions:

The verse calls us to put away "childish things." What specific immature attitudes, words, or behaviors do you still struggle with? How is it impacting your life and Christian walk?

_____
_____
_____
_____
_____
_____
_____
_____

Reflect on your recent words and thoughts—do they reflect a child-like reaction or a Christ-like response? What is one area you need to grow in this week?

_____
_____
_____
_____
_____
_____
_____
_____

What specific cultural messages have influenced your view of manhood, and how does Scripture challenge or correct those views?

_____
_____
_____
_____
_____
_____

Refer to the list of five abilities (responsibility, accountability, availability, vulnerability, and power) every man of God needs to do what seems impossible. What stood out to you about each one, and why? In what areas do you see the greatest need for refinement?

_____
_____
_____
_____
_____

Think about someone who looks up to you—whether at home, work, or church. What is one specific way you can model spiritual or emotional maturity for that person this week?

_____
_____
_____
_____
_____
_____

In which of the three areas (spiritual, relational, emotional) do you find it most difficult to mature? Why do you think that is, and what needs to happen to change it?

_____
_____
_____
_____
_____
_____
_____
_____

Complete the "Am I Maturing as a Man?" exercise at the end of this chapter. What did you discover, and how do you plan to move forward in maturing in specific areas of your life?

_____
_____
_____
_____
_____
_____
_____
_____

Icebreaker: Childish vs. Christ-like—Share a moment when you reacted immaturely to a situation. How would you handle it differently now as a more mature man of God?

Discussion Tips: See "How to Use This Study Guide" for general guidelines.
- Discuss how maturity is a process, not a one-time event.
- Challenge the group to evaluate if they are growing in maturity, or are stagnant?

Closing Challenge: Identify one immature attitude, reaction, or habit that you need to put away this week. Take one practical step toward spiritual, emotional, or relational maturity and check in next time.

CHAPTER 8

KNOW WHO YOU ARE

God's love defines you, and nothing can change that.

READING TIME

As you read Chapter 8: "Know Who You Are" in *The Way of the Marksmen*, review, reflect on, and respond to the text by answering the following questions.

REVIEW, REFLECT, AND RESPOND

How has the world's skewed definition of manhood influenced the way you view and define your own identity as a man?

_____
_____
_____
_____
_____
_____
_____
_____
_____

The chapter emphasizes that your identity is not tied to performance but to God's grace. What areas of your life are still driven by a need to prove your worth, and why?

_____
_____
_____
_____
_____
_____
_____
_____
_____

> "For if you listen to the word and don't obey, it is like glancing at your face in a mirror. You see yourself, walk away, and forget what you look like."
>
> —James 1:23-24 (NLT)

Consider the scripture above and answer the following questions:

How is James's mirror analogy relevant to our struggle with seeing ourselves as God sees us?

___

___

___

___

___

___

___

___

According to this scripture, how is disobedience tied to the fallible ways we view ourselves?

___

___

___

___

___

___

___

___

Who do you spend the most time with? Who are you becoming as a result of that, and how closely does it mirror God's character? What specific Scripture can you rely on to counteract that lie?

What are the most common lies you tell yourself, and how have they shaped the way you view yourself?

Reflect on a moment when you felt fully confident in your identity as a child of God. What was happening during that time, and how can you create habits that remind you of this truth regularly?

_____
_____
_____
_____
_____

How would you describe your current level of intimacy with God, and how does it shape your understanding of your identity?

_____
_____
_____
_____
_____

Review the three common barriers (comparison, past mistakes, worldly definitions of success) to knowing who you are. Which resonates with you the most, and why?

_____
_____
_____
_____

_____
_____

Complete the "Do You Know Who You Are in Christ?" exercise at the end of this chapter. What did you discover, and how do you plan to move forward in embracing and living out your identity in Christ?

_____
_____
_____
_____
_____

Icebreaker: Mirror Reflection—Share a time when you believed something about yourself that wasn't true. How did God reveal the truth about your identity to you?

Discussion Tips: See "How to Use This Study Guide" for general guidelines.

- Discuss how culture, comparison, and past mistakes distort our identity.
- Encourage the group to reflect on how Scripture defines their worth.

Closing Challenge: Identify one lie or false belief you've been holding about yourself. Find a Bible verse that speaks to your true identity in Christ, meditate on it this week, and check in next time.

CHAPTER 9

BE LIKE JESUS

> We don't have time to leave things unsaid or delay what God calls us to do.

READING TIME

As you read Chapter 9: "Be Like Jesus" in *The Way of the Marksmen*, review, reflect on, and respond to the text by answering the following questions.

REVIEW, REFLECT, AND RESPOND

Think of a specific moment where pride caused you to prioritize yourself over someone else. What did that reveal about your heart at the time?

_____
_____
_____
_____
_____
_____
_____
_____

Jesus loved even those who rejected or betrayed Him. Reflect on someone who has deeply hurt or disappointed you. How willing are you to forgive them and show them love, and what would it cost you?

_____
_____
_____
_____
_____
_____
_____
_____

> "We know that we have come to know him if we keep his commands. Whoever says, 'I know him,' but does not do what he commands is a liar, and the truth is not in that person. But if anyone obeys his word, love for God is truly made complete in them. This is how we know we are in him: Whoever claims to live in him must live as Jesus did."
>
> —1 John 2:3-6 (NIV)

Consider the scripture above and answer the following questions:

The verse says, *"Those who say they live in God should live their lives as Jesus did."* In what specific ways does your life reflect Jesus's character, and in what areas do you feel convicted to grow?

_____
_____
_____
_____
_____
_____

The passage calls out those who claim to know God but fail to live in obedience. Reflect on the consistency between your words and actions. Where are the discrepancies? How can you begin to close that gap?

_____
_____
_____
_____
_____
_____

Reflect on a decision or habit where you've compromised your obedience to Christ to avoid discomfort or loss. How has this affected your relationship with God, and what stops you from surrendering fully now?

_____

_____

_____

_____

_____

_____

_____

_____

_____

To what degree do you find yourself doubting the magnitude of your influence on others? What underlying beliefs or experiences might be contributing to this doubt?

_____

_____

_____

_____

_____

_____

_____

_____

_____

What stood out about the three barriers (pride, selfishness, fear) to being like Jesus? Do you find any of them interfere with your ability to reflect the heart and mind of Jesus? How so?

_____
_____
_____
_____
_____
_____
_____
_____

Have you delayed doing what God has called you to do? Why? What consequences—spiritual, relational, or otherwise—might your delay in obeying God's call already be causing

_____
_____
_____
_____
_____
_____
_____
_____

Complete the "Am I Becoming More Like Jesus?" measurement check at the end of this chapter. What did you discover, and how will you strive to become more like Christ?

_____
_____
_____
_____
_____
_____
_____
_____
_____

Icebreaker: Living Like Jesus—Share a time when you had the opportunity to reflect Jesus's character but struggled to do so. What did you learn from that experience?

Discussion Tips: See "How to Use This Study Guide" for general guidelines.
- Talk about how daily habits shape whether we reflect Christ.
- Challenge the group to think about where their actions and their faith are not aligned?

Closing Challenge: Identify one area of pride, selfishness, or fear that is holding you back from fully following Jesus. Take a step this week to act in obedience where you've previously hesitated, and check in next time.

PART 3

THE CHARACTER OF A MARKSMAN

CHAPTER 10

MEN OF INTEGRITY

> Too many of us are content with being somewhat reliable, but as men striving to reflect Christ, we must aim higher.

READING TIME

As you read Chapter 10: "Men of Integrity" in *The Way of the Marksmen*, review, reflect on, and respond to the text by answering the following questions.

REVIEW, REFLECT, AND RESPOND

Reflect on an area of your life where you feel there's a disconnect between your private and public self. What specific behavior or habit needs to change to bring your life into alignment with biblical principles of integrity?

_____
_____
_____
_____
_____
_____
_____
_____

Think of a recent situation where you compromised your values for convenience, gain, or approval. What was the immediate result, and what did it reveal about where your heart was focused?

_____
_____
_____
_____
_____
_____
_____
_____

> "People with integrity walk safely, but those who follow crooked paths will be exposed."
>
> —Proverbs 10:9 (NLT)

Consider the scripture above and answer the following questions:

Are there any hidden compromises or sins in your life that you need to confront before they are exposed and cause greater harm? What is the initial action you can take to address this issue before it escalates further?

_____
_____
_____
_____
_____
_____
_____
_____

Why do you think this verse ties integrity to safety?

_____
_____
_____
_____
_____
_____
_____
_____

How do you respond to difficult situations or conversations? Do you confront them or run away from them? Provide examples. What factors contributed to your response?

How much trust do those closest to you place in you, and what do you believe has contributed to that level of trust?

Think about a time when you chose to do what was right, even though you could have avoided consequences by doing what was wrong. How did that decision shape your character, and what lasting impact has it had on your life today?

_____
_____
_____
_____
_____
_____

Integrity requires accountability. Who in your life has permission to call you out when your actions fall short of your values?

_____
_____
_____
_____
_____
_____

How consistently do you demonstrate your integrity, even in the smallest of actions? Provide an example. Do you think those who know you best would affirm your answer?

_____
_____
_____

_____
_____
_____

Living with transparency requires vulnerability. In what specific area of your life have you avoided being fully open with others, and what is holding you back from bringing that into the light?

_____
_____
_____
_____
_____

Icebreaker: The Integrity Test—Share a time when you had to choose between doing what was right and what was easy. What did you decide, and what was the outcome?

Discussion Tips: See "How to Use This Study Guide" for general guidelines.
- Discuss why integrity isn't just about big decisions but small, everyday choices.
- Challenge the group: Are you the same person in private as you are in public?

Closing Challenge: Identify one area where your private and public self need to align more closely. Take an intentional step this week to live with greater integrity and check in next time.

CHAPTER 11

MEN OF HUMILITY

> In the Bible, humility is not about thinking less of yourself but rather thinking of yourself less.

READING TIME

As you read Chapter 11: "Men of Humility" in *The Way of the Marksmen*, review, reflect on, and respond to the text by answering the following questions.

REVIEW, REFLECT, AND RESPOND

Reflect on an area of your life where pride has caused you to push forward alone instead of seeking God's help. What was the outcome, and what adjustments have you made?

_____
_____
_____
_____
_____
_____
_____
_____

Think of a recent conflict where you struggled to apologize or take responsibility. What stopped you from humbling yourself, and how might the relationship have been impacted if you had responded differently?

_____
_____
_____
_____
_____
_____
_____
_____

> "Don't be selfish; don't try to impress others. Be humble, thinking of others as better than yourselves. Don't look out only for your own interests, but take an interest in others, too."
>
> —Philippians 2:3-4 [NLT]

Consider the scripture above and answer the following questions:

In what relationship or situation have you prioritized your desires over someone else's needs? How does this reveal areas where humility is still a struggle?

_____
_____
_____
_____
_____
_____

In what area of your life do you catch yourself seeking recognition or trying to impress others? What specific change can you make to approach that area with greater humility?

_____
_____
_____
_____
_____
_____

Think of a time when a "humble brag" has disguised itself as true humility. How does the biblical understanding of humility contrast with the concept of a "humble brag"?

Who in your life might you consider "beneath" you, and what would it look like for you to serve them selflessly?

Reflect on the statement, *"God will humble you when you least expect."* Have you ever experienced this? Why do you think these moments often take us by surprise?

_____
_____
_____
_____
_____
_____

Who in your life do you actively seek feedback from? Do you wait for it, or do you ask for it? If you were to implement this practice right now, what would it look like?

_____
_____
_____
_____
_____
_____

How well do you handle criticism or rejection? Explain your answer.

_____
_____
_____

_____
_____
_____

How consistently do you practice gratitude in your daily life? What specific blessings can you thank God for right now?

_____
_____
_____
_____
_____
_____

Icebreaker: Lesson in Humility—Share a time when God humbled you in an unexpected way. What did you learn from that experience?

Discussion Tips: See "How to Use This Study Guide" for general guidelines.
- Discuss how true humility is not weakness but strength under control.
- Challenge the group to consider if they serve to seek recognition, or are content serving quietly?

Closing Challenge: Identify one area where pride is holding you back from fully surrendering to God or serving others selflessly. Take a step this week to practice humility in that area and check in next time.

CHAPTER 12.

MEN OF COURAGE

Running from difficult situations
only makes things worse.

READING TIME

As you read Chapter 12: "Men of Courage" in *The Way of the Marksmen*, review, reflect on, and respond to the text by answering the following questions.

REVIEW, REFLECT, AND RESPOND

In your own words, how would you describe biblical courage? How well do you embody biblical courage?

_____
_____
_____
_____
_____
_____
_____
_____

Think about a recent decision where you hesitated to act because you couldn't guarantee success. What might have changed if you had moved forward in faith rather than waiting for certainty?

_____
_____
_____
_____
_____
_____
_____
_____

> "This is my command—be strong and courageous! Do not be afraid or discouraged. For the Lord your God is with you wherever you go."
>
> —Joshua 1:9 (NLT)

Consider the scripture above and answer the following questions:

How does this truth impact the way you view the challenges you're currently facing? Are you relying on His presence, or are you trying to face these challenges in your own strength?

_____
_____
_____
_____
_____
_____
_____

Why do you think God commands courage rather than suggests it? What does this imply about your responsibility to step into His calling despite your fears?

_____
_____
_____
_____
_____
_____
_____

Has your courage ever been tested? What did you do well, and what would you have done differently?

When have you let fear push you to conform to the pressures and patterns of this world? What was that like, and how did God redirect you to stand firm on your values against opposition?

Why shouldn't the fear of failure stop you from taking bold steps of obedience toward the place God is directing you to go?

What kind of man do you want to be? What does that look like in your ministry, your family, your work, and other important areas of your life? Where does courage fit into that vision?

_____
_____
_____
_____
_____
_____
_____
_____

In what area of your life is God calling you to step out in courage during this season? What fears are coming up for you, and what steps can you take to deepen your faith and rely more fully on God as you face the challenges ahead?

_____
_____
_____
_____
_____
_____
_____
_____

How will you implement the steps outlined at the end of this chapter to face the current challenges in your life with greater courage?

_____
_____
_____
_____
_____
_____
_____
_____
_____

Icebreaker: A Time to Be Bold—Share a moment when you had to make a difficult decision that required courage. How did you handle it, and what was the outcome?

Discussion Tips: See "How to Use This Study Guide" for general guidelines.
- Discuss why courage is often about obedience rather than confidence.
- Challenge the group to reflect on what fears are keeping them from stepping into what God has called them to do?

Closing Challenge: Identify one fear or hesitation that has been holding you back. Take one bold step this week to trust God and act in courage rather than waiting for certainty. Check in next time.

CHAPTER 13

MEN OF COMPASSION

> The person who is against you today can become your brother tomorrow.

READING TIME

As you read Chapter 13: "Men of Compassion" in *The Way of the Marksmen*, review, reflect on, and respond to the text by answering the following questions.

REVIEW, REFLECT, AND RESPOND

How easily do you find it to act compassionately towards those who are difficult to love? What specific attitudes or beliefs make it harder for you to show compassion to those individuals?

_____
_____
_____
_____
_____
_____
_____

How is biblical compassion different than human compassion? In what ways have you relied on your feelings rather than God's call when deciding whether to act compassionately?

_____
_____
_____
_____
_____
_____
_____

> "And you must love the Lord your God with all your heart, all your soul, all your mind, and all your strength. The second is equally important: 'Love your neighbor as yourself.' No other commandment is greater than these."
>
> —Mark 12: 30-31 (NLT)

Consider the scripture above and answer the following questions:

Jesus places equal importance on loving God and loving others. Reflect on your life—does one commandment come more naturally to you than the other? Why or why not?

_____
_____
_____
_____
_____
_____
_____
_____

Why do you think loving God and loving your neighbor must work in tandem?

_____
_____
_____
_____
_____
_____
_____
_____

Who in your life might feel unseen or undervalued, and how can you intentionally show them the love of Christ?

_____
_____
_____
_____
_____
_____

How compassionate are you towards yourself? How do you think that transfers to your relationships with others, and more importantly, to your relationship with God?

_____
_____
_____
_____
_____
_____

What are your most profound struggles with demonstrating compassion as a man in today's culture?

_____
_____
_____
_____
_____
_____

How easily does vulnerability come to you? How do you view vulnerability, and in what ways has it impacted your relationships (either its presence or absence)?

_____
_____
_____
_____
_____
_____
_____
_____

What barriers can you identify that may be hindering you from developing and demonstrating compassion for others or someone specific?

_____
_____
_____
_____
_____
_____
_____
_____

Where has unforgiveness taken root in your heart, and what can you do today to begin the process of forgiveness?

_____
_____
_____
_____
_____
_____
_____
_____
_____

Icebreaker: Loving the Unlovable—Share a time when you struggled to show compassion to someone difficult. What was holding you back, and how did you eventually respond?

Discussion Tips: See "How to Use This Study Guide" for general guidelines.
- Discuss how biblical compassion is an action, not just a feeling.
- Challenge the group: Who is God calling you to show compassion to, even when it's hard?

Closing Challenge: Identify one person in your life who needs compassion, even if they are difficult to love. Take a step this week to show them kindness intentionally, and check in next time.

CHAPTER 14

MEN OF FAITH

As marksmen consistently aim for their targets, we must be resilient and push ourselves to endure.

READING TIME

As you read Chapter 14: "Men of Faith" in *The Way of the Marksmen*, review, reflect on, and respond to the text by answering the following questions.

REVIEW, REFLECT, AND RESPOND

Which areas of your life present the greatest challenge when it comes to maintaining commitment?

_____
_____
_____
_____
_____
_____
_____
_____
_____

Think about a recent challenge where you were tempted to give up. How did you respond, and what did you learn about your faithfulness?

_____
_____
_____
_____
_____
_____
_____
_____
_____

> "Let love and faithfulness never leave you; bind them around your neck, write them on the tablet of your heart."
>
> —Proverbs 3:3 (NIV)

Consider the scripture above and answer the following questions:

In what ways does this scripture challenge you? What does the imagery used in this verse tell you about the message of remaining faithful?

_____
_____
_____
_____
_____
_____
_____

In what ways do love and faithfulness go hand-in-hand?

_____
_____
_____
_____
_____
_____
_____

Think about a moment when you faced the greatest pressure you've ever experienced. How did you persevere, and what was the outcome? How has it influenced the way you respond to internal and external pressures today?

Think about a responsibility or relationship where you've struggled to remain committed because it challenges your insecurities. How does avoiding this responsibility or relationship align with—or conflict with—your desire to live faithfully for God?

The chapter warns that options can become the enemy of success. Reflect on a time when having too many choices led you to hesitate or quit. How can removing certain "exit strategies" help you commit more fully to what God has called you to do?

Reflecting on the highs and lows of your life, what have you observed about the way they have shaped your character, and how does this encourage you to remain steadfast in your faithfulness?

_____
_____
_____
_____
_____
_____
_____
_____

The chapter emphasizes that being faithful to small things builds character for larger responsibilities. Reflect on a daily task or responsibility you tend to neglect. How can faithfully approaching it transform your outlook and testimony?

_____
_____
_____
_____
_____
_____
_____
_____

Are you a man of your word? Where might you fall short, and what can you do to rectify it?

_____
_____
_____
_____
_____
_____
_____
_____
_____

Icebreaker: Staying the Course—Share a time when you wanted to give up on something important. What helped you stay committed, or what do you wish you had done differently?

Discussion Tips: See "How to Use This Study Guide" for general guidelines.
- Discuss how faithfulness is developed through trials, not ease.
- Challenge the group: Are you faithful in the small things, or only when it's easy?

Closing Challenge: Identify one area in your life where you need to grow in faithfulness—whether in relationships, responsibilities, or spiritual commitment. Take one intentional step this week to remain steadfast, and check in next time.

CHAPTER 15

IT ALL COMES TOGETHER

The amazing thing about following Jesus is that there is no perfect cookie-cutter system.

READING TIME

As you read Chapter 15: "It All Comes Together" in *The Way of the Marksmen*, review, reflect on, and respond to the text by answering the following questions.

REVIEW, REFLECT, AND RESPOND

What knowledge and wisdom have you gained from your journey walking with Christ, and what are you doing with them?

_____
_____
_____
_____
_____
_____
_____
_____
_____

Legacy is a central theme in this chapter. What kind of spiritual legacy are you building for those who come after you? How do your daily actions reflect or contradict the legacy you hope to leave?

_____
_____
_____
_____
_____
_____
_____
_____
_____

> "I planted the seed, Apollos watered it, but God has been making it grow. So neither the one who plants nor the one who waters is anything, but only God, who makes things grow."
>
> —1 Corinthians 3:6-7 (NIV)

Consider the scripture above and answer the following questions:

What seeds are you planting in your own life to become the marksman that God has called you to be? Are they moving you closer to the target or pushing you further away?

_____
_____
_____
_____
_____
_____
_____
_____

Who in your life are you intentionally pouring into, and how does this align with the calling God has given you?

_____
_____
_____
_____
_____
_____
_____
_____

This chapter encourages men to find reminders that keep them focused on Jesus. What specific visual, auditory, or written reminders could you incorporate into your daily life to stay grounded in your faith?

_____
_____
_____
_____
_____
_____
_____
_____
_____
_____

Rest is a critical component of a faithful life. Reflect on your current balance of work and rest. Does it demonstrate good stewardship of what God has entrusted to you?

_____
_____
_____
_____
_____
_____
_____
_____
_____
_____

Have you ever felt like the path you're on is taking you further from your purpose rather than closer to it? How might reframing your perspective to trust God's plan help you see this season as a necessary part of His greater purpose for your life?

_____
_____
_____
_____
_____

Where in your life have you hesitated to lead, and what is holding you back from stepping fully into that role?

_____
_____
_____
_____
_____

What have you learned about the importance of becoming a marksman?

_____
_____
_____

_____
_____
_____

Reflect on a lesson from this book that convicted you the most. How will you apply it to your life in a way that creates real change?

_____
_____
_____
_____
_____
_____

Icebreaker: Legacy Check—If someone were to describe your spiritual legacy today, what would they say? Is that the legacy you want to leave behind?

Discussion Tips: See "How to Use This Study Guide" for general guidelines.
- Discuss why spiritual legacy isn't about perfection but consistency.
- Challenge the group to think: Are you planting the right seeds in your life and the lives of others?

Closing Challenge: Reflect on one key lesson from this book that has challenged you the most. Take a specific step this week to apply it to your life in a lasting way, and check in next time.

www.ingramcontent.com/pod-product-compliance
Lightning Source LLC
Chambersburg PA
CBHW070049100426
42734CB00040B/2899